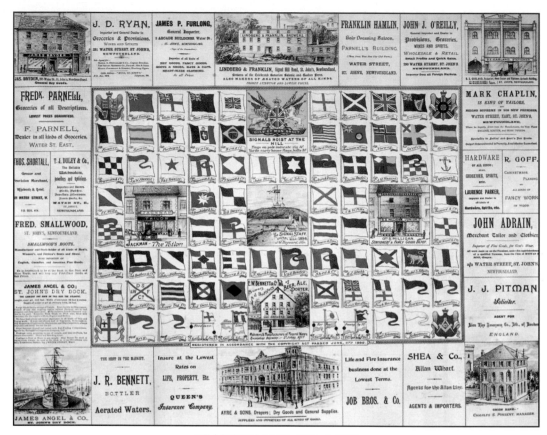

HAYWARD FLAGS

This 1894 Code of Signals, bordered by advertisements of prominent St. John's businesses, is the work of John William Hayward (1843-1913). Hayward, a self-taught St. John's artist of note, produced many similar charts for local companies and sponsors. To this day, they chronicle the activity of a busy Atlantic seaport and commerce centre. For almost three centuries, Signal Hill functioned as the communications centre for the port of St. John's. Although at first the emphasis was placed on warning the community of the approach of warships (friendly or hostile), it was the commercial shipping that eventually became the most important part of the signalling system. Each St. John's company which operated trading vessels had its own "house flag." As a ship approached the harbour, its house flag and ship number would be raised on the signal mast at Cape Spear and repeated by the station on Signal Hill. The merchant downtown thus would have time to prepare for the arrival of his ship.

SIGNAL HILL

An Illustrated History

Newfoundland Historic Parks Association

Signal Hill National Historic Park

ISBN# 0-919735-02-9

Reprinted in 1997 by the Newfoundland Historic Parks Association
P.O. Box 5542
St. John's, Newfoundland
A1C 5W4

This book was written and produced by Amy Zierler and Cam Mustard from research by Parks Canada historians James Candow and Jean-Pierre Proulx, and by Paul O'Neill, Marilyn Dawe and A.F. King.

ACKNOWLEDGEMENTS

Newfoundland Historic Trust Members: Pamela Murphy, Ted Rowe, Paul O'Neill

Parks Canada Staff: Edna Hall, Mary Devine, Valerie Tubman

Special thanks for assistance: John Maunder and Tony Murphy, Department of Culture, Recreation and Youth; James Candow, Parks Canada

Imagine the first ship, scanning the rough shores for a harbour. From out at sea the cliffs appear impenetrable, but somewhere they must yield an entrance against the winds. The passage discovered is a mere 400 yards wide, and narrows by half before opening into a deep, mile-long basin. The headlands on either side plunge sharply, several hundred feet, to the water's edge.

As it widens, the harbour turns west and so shelters itself behind the persistent ridge which takes the worst blows of the sea. Opposite the ridge the inland side of the harbour rises more gently, although the slopes are steep enough that hills and heights will come to characterize the city which is to be built on them over the next few hundred years.

The focus of this book is the spectacular headland which forms the north wall of the narrows. Its weather-resistant rock formed over hundreds of millions of years as the debris of ancient volcanoes swept towards the sea. Its bald rock peaks, deep valleys and ponds were crafted by the last glacier, gouging and polishing and moving boulders as it crept over the land.

The hills are not as barren as they first appear. Hundreds of species of plants have taken root among the sandstone and gravel: blueberries, partridgeberries, marshberries, crowberries, dwarf larch and juniper, wild cherry, and sedges. In summer the land blooms pink and white and purple with sheep laurel, wild rhododendron, leatherleaf and Labrador tea. As the first ship maneuvers past the cliffs, a good tree cover of white spruce, fir and alder still protects the hill's fragile topsoil.

Its natural vantage over both the sea and the harbour will make the hill a vital arm of the town which is to grow up in its shadow. It will be protector, messenger and refuge. Families, soldiers and signalmen will make their homes on the heights, ploughing fields, growing vegetables, raising sheep and cattle.

Signal Hill, as it will come to be known, will be scarped, quarried, blasted, cut over , fought over and burned. Its green and red sandstone—"of so intractable a nature," a geologist is to write, "that the action of the weather seems to have no appreciable effect whatever upon it"—will end up as part of churches, hospitals, memorials and other grand and not-so-grand buildings.

But human uses cannot ever dominate Signal Hill. With the elements for allies, the hill resists every effort to tame it. Sentries are frozen to death at their posts in the vicious storms of winter. Fierce winds—too strong to stand up in—foil chimney building engineers. Miners are frustrated by the stubborn rock. Access is a continuing problem: it will be 300 years from the time the first Europeans are known to have arrived before a proper road is cut to the summit.

None of this can happen, however, until that first ship sails through the narrows.

St. Brendan and his fellow monks

Early navigation techniques

To early Europeans, the ocean to the west was the edge of the world. There were tales of mysterious lands beyond, but it required a tremendous faith to set out for them as did, according to legend, St. Brendan and his fellow monks. They reached the promised land beyond the Atlantic, so the story goes, sometime before 600 A.D. and after seven years at sea sailed home to Ireland.

Rudimentary navigation techniques, relying on the sun, stars and currents, made successful voyages across the Atlantic unlikely, but the detail of some of the old legends, in particular the Viking sagas, led historians to believe Europeans had in fact visited "the new world" long before the great wave of exploration at the start of the 16th century.

That belief was verified in 1961 when a Norwegian couple, Helge and Anne Stine Ingstad, found the site of a 1,000-year-old Viking settlement at L'Anse aux Meadows, on the northern tip of the island of Newfoundland. Archaeological evidence shows that Vikings lived on the grassy meadow above a shallow cove for perhaps 25 years, building at least seven sod structures and forging local bog iron in a primitive smithy. As very few artifacts turned up at the site, it appears that the Vikings packed their household goods into their shallow, high-prowed ships and moved home or on to another as yet undiscovered place.

European explorers who made it to Newfoundland were not coming, as they may have thought, to an uninhabited land. Eskimo and Indian peoples moved into Newfoundland and Labrador from the west up to 9,000 years ago, and several cultures came and went long before the Vikings sailed into L'Anse aux Meadows.

The Beothucks, who probably descended from Newfoundland's early Indians, became victims of European expansion. It has been estimated that the Beothucks numbered less than 2,000 at their peak. They may have already been in decline when Europeans began exploiting the Newfoundland fishing grounds, around the year 1500. Struggling with disease and hostilities, the Indians survived another three centuries.

Most of the year they lived in the rich marine environment of eastern Newfoundland. They caught fish, seals, sea birds and shellfish and travelled in bark canoes. In early winter they moved inland to hunt caribou, beaver, ptarmigan and hare for food and skins. But as European settlement spread into the northeastern bays, the Beothucks were forced to spend more time inland where food was less plentiful. Facing starvation, their resistance to disease further

John Cabot

weakened, and still prey to attacks by settlers, the Beothucks dwindled to a tiny, desperate group by the early 19th century. A woman named Shanawdithit, believed to have been the last of her people, died of tuberculosis in June, 1829.

In 1497, King Henry VII of England gave the Italian explorer John Cabot his support *"to seeke out, discover, and finde whatsoever isles, countreyes, regions or provinces of the heathen and infidelles, whatsoever they bee, and in what part of the world soever they be, whiche before this time have beene unknown to all Christians."*

Cabot did not find the land of spices he sought. Oriental spices, especially pepper, cloves and nutmeg, were in great demand in Europe; used to disguise the taste of spoiled meat, they were household necessities, not luxuries. But he did find something which not only was equally vital to the economy of Europe, but would also chart the course of Newfoundland for the next 500 years: fish.

No detailed record of Cabot's voyage has been found and we do not know exactly where he landed, but on his return to England he reported: "The sea is covered with fish which are caught not merely with nets, but with baskets, a stone being attached to make the basket sink into the water."

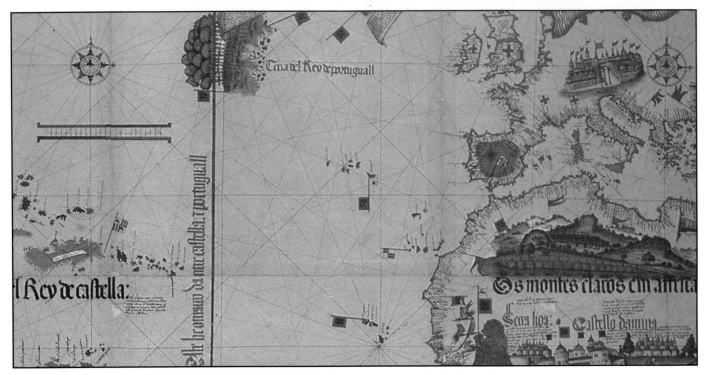

Whether Cabot first landed at Cape Bonavista or Cape Breton, the fishing grounds he spoke of were almost certainly off the coast of Newfoundland. News of his discovery spread quickly through Europe and by the turn of the century, ships from Spain, Portugal, France and England were making regular trips across the North Atlantic to fish in these barely charted waters.

This Portuguese map, dated 1502, is one of the earliest to show Newfoundland. With only a small stretch of the eastern Avalon Peninsula depicted, the island appears as "Tera del Rey del portugall"—Land of the King of Portugal. It was a Portuguese explorer, Gaspar Corte Real, who is credited with naming St. John's on his 1501 voyage to the new-found land, and it was not long before its excellent

deep harbour became the centre of activity for the international fishery underway every summer offshore.

The island provided a welcome refuge from a summer storm and a convenient place to carry out repairs, but in winter, as English geographer Richard Hakluyt wrote, St. John's was "given over to the fruition of birds and wild animals."

Towards spring every year,

European ports like Lisbon, one of the great mercantile centres of the 16th century, scrambled to prepare their fleets for the lucrative fishery three thousand miles away. Although the English would come to monopolize the Newfoundland fishery by the end of the century, they were at first vastly outnumbered by other countries. On his fourth voyage to Newfoundland in 1578, Bristol merchant Anthony Parkhurst observed, "There were generally more than 100 sail of Spaniards taking cod, and from 20 to 30 killing whales; 50 sails of Portuguese; 150 sail of French and Bretons mostly very small; but of the English only 50 sails."

With a fishing season from April to October, and one month's crossing time at either end, fishing crews could spend eight months or more at sea without ever going ashore.

At the banks the captain shortened sail and each fisherman placed himself in a small barrel hung over the side of the vessel. Suspended above the waves and wearing a large leather apron which hung over the barrel to keep him dry, he fished with a long, heavily-weighted line. In a good day's fishing, a man might take in 100 cod.

As the fisherman in the barrel took a cod, he passed it up to the deck of the ship where it was gutted and trussed, then tossed into the hold. There it was salted and piled while the blood and water ran out of it. After 48 hours the fish were piled again between layers of salt. They would keep in this way without spoiling until delivery in Europe months later.

The thick white flesh of the cod, rich in protein without being fatty, is easily and effectively cured by salting and drying. Countries with an abundance of salt, especially France, Portugal and Spain, practised what is called the green fishery. Loaded with salt when they left port in January or February, their vessels were stacked with cod when they returned.

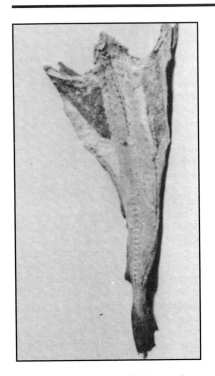

England did not become active in the fishery across the Atlantic until the 1570's, when competition with Denmark in the rich waters off Iceland forced her to turn to Newfoundland. Lacking the huge supplies of salt required to pursue the simple green fishery, the English dried their cod in the sun on the shores of the island, in protected harbours such as St. John's.

In the dry fishery, men worked the waters close to shore, returning every evening to clean and split the day's catch on a wharf, called a stage. Each fish was brushed with salt, just enough to keep it from spoiling until it was ready for drying. A few days later, the cod was washed in water and laid out on frames, called flakes, to dry in the air and sun. The elaborate drying process, requiring much skill, took several weeks altogether, and the finished product had to be kept dry during the long trip back to England.

The shore-based dry fishery meant English fishermen, unlike their European counterparts, actually lived in Newfoundland for the summer months. Because the building of stages, flakes and shelters every spring cut into lucrative fishing time, the merchants of West Country ports who controlled the fishery sometimes placed men in Newfoundland to maintain the structures through the harsh winter.

Sir Humphrey Gilbert is often called the "Father of British Colonisation," but when he sailed through the Narrows in August, 1583, to claim Terra Nova in the name of Queen Elizabeth I, there were 36 ships of various nations in St. John's harbour. The Queen had reluctantly granted letters patent to this eager soldier-adventurer, and accompanied by a band of musicians he had brought from England, Gilbert went ashore, climbed a hill, and ceremoniously took possession of all he surveyed.

Like others in his day, Gilbert had long dreamed of a voyage to discover a northwest passage to China. He planned to establish English colonies in the New World along the way, but Sir Humphrey and his ship went down in a storm on his way back to England, not three weeks after leaving St. John's.

With promoters like Gilbert and his half-brother Sir Walter Raleigh, both of whom had the ear of Queen Elizabeth, the idea that England should control North America began to take hold towards the end of the 16th century. Newfoundland, where the continent began, suddenly became an area of strategic importance to England. Controlling Newfoundland meant ruling the seas. This is what the Royal Navy set out to do.

In 1585, Sir Bernard Drake made a devastating attack on the Spanish fleet at Newfoundland. With the defeat of the Spanish Armada three years later, all nations recognised England's rising naval power, and French and Spanish fishing vessels retreated to the south coast of Newfoundland and into the Gulf of St. Lawrence. The struggle between England and France was to last the better part of the next two centuries.

Newfoundland cod was a highly prized commodity on the European market by the beginning of the 17th century, at least as important to the intricate trading economy as the Canadian fur trade. As England pushed other countries out of Newfoundland waters, those countries became markets for English fish. During the reign of Elizabeth I (1558-1603), the fisheries employed some 10,000 people and brought in £500,000 a year, more than half of England's total national revenue.

There was another reason the English government supported the fishing industry. Fishermen who had to make long ocean voyages became skilled seamen who could man the ships of the Royal Navy in time of war.

But official England continued to resist efforts by some to settle in Newfoundland. While the seasonal fishing bases of the West Country merchants were evolving into permanent settlements, the merchants sometimes brutally opposed settlement as a threat to their exclusive domain. The government agreed with them that England could protect its interests from the seas and did not move to fortify the island.

Sir Humphrey Gilbert

France was the first country to garrison part of Newfoundland. While the English merchants and the planters, as those who advocated settlement were called, argued about how best to protect England's fishing interests, the French established a colony at Plaisance (Placentia today), 80 miles across the Avalon Peninsula from St. John's.

In 1662, King Louis XIV sent Nicholas Gargot to establish a colonial government at Plaisance. The governor built forts and successfully encouraged settlement of the excellent harbours around Placentia Bay. In choosing this area to fortify, the French also gained an advantage in the fishing trade. The field ice which blocks most Newfoundland harbours in early spring does not generally reach the south coast. French ships using Plaisance as their base could get a head start on the fishery and make deliveries to European markets several months before the English.

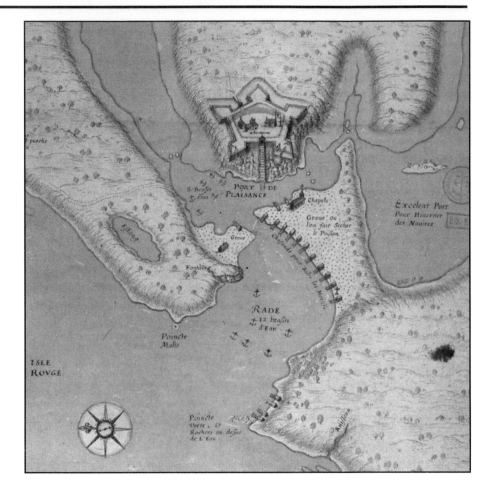

In 1610, over the protests of the West Country merchants, John Guy of the London and Bristol Company was granted a charter to establish the first British colony in Newfoundland. Although he had agreed not to interfere with the seasonal fishing operations, the home port merchants made sure the migratory fishermen saw the colonists as their enemies. They coexisted uneasily for several seasons, but after some of his buildings at Cupid Cove were burned, Guy returned to England in 1613, discouraged.

The prospering French colony at Plaisance forced England to revise its policy towards settlement. After 1677, when Parliament rescinded a law calling for the deportation of settlers from Newfoundland, planters were tolerated—but still not protected. About 350 families in modest settlements, from Trepassey on the Avalon coast to Bay de Verde at the mouth of Conception Bay, looked after their own defense. They built crude forts and earthworks and scrounged guns. A network of trails cut through the forest linked the settlements to St. John's, their "capital."

Repeated petitions from residents of Newfoundland could not convince the home government of the need to erect costly land defenses.

John Guy

The capture of St. John's by the French in 1696

Having complete confidence in the supremacy of her navy, England did not believe St. John's could be attacked by land.

In the summer of 1696, by using two small, hastily constructed forts at strategic points in the Narrows, the planters successfully repulsed a French fleet trying to enter the harbour. But that winter French troops advanced on St. John's again, this time by land, across the barren interior to the Avalon Peninsula.

The residents retreated to a new work called King William's Fort which they had built on a height of land at the east end of the harbour, but they surrendered after two days of resistance.

The victorious French razed the entire settlement and spent the rest of the winter sacking fishing settlements on Conception Bay. When Colonel John Gibson, dispatched from England with 1,500 men, arrived in St. John's a few months later, he "found nothing but destruction and ruine, not a house standing but one."

St. John's "grew up wild and ungoverned," writes historian Paul O'Neill of his native city. The early planters kept cattle, sheep, pigs, and horses, grew vegetables and caught fish, but they lived in a lawless frontier, in danger from enemies and countrymen alike.

Newfoundland's unsecured harbours were as attractive to pirates and roving privateers as they were to fishing captains. Several pirates made Newfoundland settlements their base for forays into the Caribbean where they intercepted European ships loaded with booty from the plundering of the ancient cities of South America. Others exacted tribute from vessels fishing on the Grand Banks. St. John's, being easily defensible, was considered to be safest from attack, but in the absence of organized defenses several privateers managed to invade it in the 17th century. "If there had been but six guns mounted in St. John's," a Dutch admiral noted in 1665, "I would not have adventured in."

In summer, the seasonal fishing crews swelled the tiny winter population. They brought with them fishing admirals, whose notorious rule lasted nearly 100 years. Beginning in 1630, the captain of the first ship to arrive in any harbour was the ruler of that harbour for the season. The fishing admirals were not military men, but they had the blessing of the king and they answered to no one. The worst are remembered as sadistic, illiterate tyrants who would flog a man to death for petty theft. Their presence did not advance the cause for civil order.

A signal cannon

The pirate Black Bart Roberts, c1700

The English troops who came to revive St. John's in the wake of the French attack left behind 350 men to winter over at the beleaguered capital. As they rebuilt Fort William and the Narrows batteries, planters who managed to escape the attack returned from their hideouts and began to rebuild their lives.

The French captured St. John's three times between 1696 and 1709, each time as part of a series of raids aimed at destroying the English fishing trade. This prolonged period of conflict, however, allowed the inhabitants of Newfoundland to become firmly entrenched. They had no competition from the migratory fishery which the dangers of wartime sea crossings and a loss of crews to the Navy had brought to a virtual standstill. The Treaty of Utrecht, signed in 1713, put all of Newfoundland under English authority. (France retained the right to fish north of Conception Bay.) The war over, the West Countrymen returned to the Newfoundland fishery, but they stuck to the offshore banks, leaving the inshore grounds to the inhabitants.

As St. John's grew, that first garrison evolved into a kind of military rule by the senior naval officer, but the fishery remained a dominant force. All around the harbour, a strip of land 200 yards wide from the high water mark was reserved exclusively for the use of the fishery.

Signal Hill served as a watch post from at least the start of the 18th century. Artillerymen stationed on the heights overlooking the ocean signalled Fort William of ships approaching the harbour. From the grim scaffolding on Gibbet Hill, the knoll just back from Signal Hill, a criminal would hang by his neck in full view of the community below, an example to others to avoid a similar fate.

View of the Narrows, 1750

The military history of Signal Hill in the 18th and 19th centuries is largely a story of unrealized plans, shifting policies, and never-ending struggle against the elements. War with France or the young American nation periodically increased the urgency for a strong garrison at St. John's, but with peace would come budget reductions and construction delays.

Signal Hill was not considered in England's first plan of defense for St. John's. Despite its command of both harbour and sea, the dramatic summit no doubt appeared too great an obstacle to defenders and attackers alike; besides, England continued to rely on the Royal Navy to prevent attacks on Newfoundland. Fort William, rebuilt largely with materials which fishing vessels brought from England each year, remained the focus of St. John's defense, although the garrison chaplain, among others, considered it "very ill situated having a Hill in front and Rear to command it."

Lieutenant-Colonel William Amherst

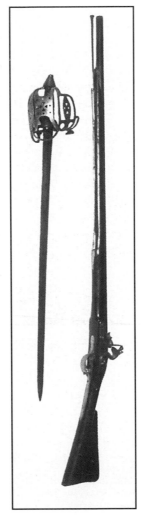

Signal Hill's strategic advantages were not recognized until the Seven Years' War—and then it was by the French. Having lost nearly all their possessions in America, the French decided to capture an English settlement in hopes of securing an advantage in the peace negotiations that were soon to take place. The poorly protected town of St. John's with its garrison of only 64 men was an ideal target. Two warships and two frigates reached St. John's on June 27, 1762. The English garrison, offering no resistance, surrendered unconditionally.

When Lieutenant Colonel William Amherst, with troops gathered from New York, Halifax, and Louisbourg, made St. John's eleven weeks later, he found the French well-entrenched. Amherst, under the command of Lord Colville, had to land further up the coast, at Torbay, and march overland to the town. As the English advanced, French troops took up position on Signal Hill and other high ground where they could fire down on them.

Amherst's victory was hard-won, and made him realize the strategic importance of fortifying Signal Hill. However, the peace treaty signed several months later put an end to plans for extensive fortifications. British defense policy again declared that "the protection of the Inhabitants settled on the Island is neither practicable nor desirable."

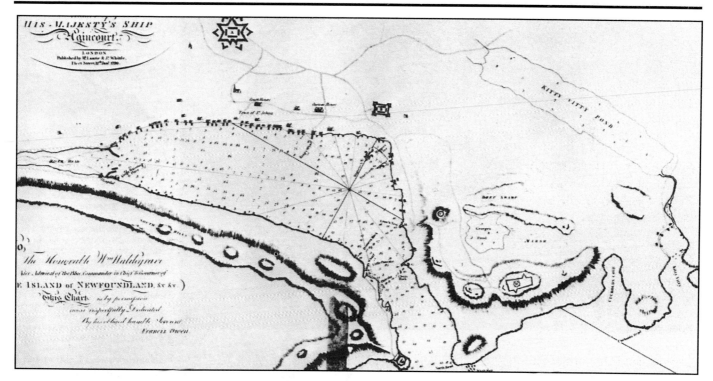

It was with the dual threats of the Napoleonic Wars (1793-1815) in Europe and the friendship between France and the United States, that Signal Hill began to play a major role in the defense of St. John's. While the batteries guarding the harbour were strengthened, England designated Signal Hill as the post of ultimate retreat for the town and garrison, "in case of a very superior enemy attacking this place."

The summits and valleys, still largely untouched, became the scene of ambitious construction activity.

In the first two years of construction (1795-1796), military builders worked on a blockhouse, officers' barracks, a storehouse, new batteries, and a masonry and wood stockade. An aborted French attack in July 1796, their final attempt on Newfoundland, furnished proof of the new importance of Signal Hill.

Deep ponds for fresh water, good spruce and fir cover for timber and firewood, and hard but quarryable sandstone at the base of Gibbet Hill aided construction of the heights. A proper road (shown on this 1798 map) was not cut until after 1796, however, and all the artillery had to be parbuckled up the cliffs from the harbour below.

View of Signal Hill and the Narrows, c1798

Amherst's Tower, 1790

"The Harbour of St. John's is the completest on the island of Newfoundland," wrote *The Times* of London in 1796. "It is entirely landlocked, perfectly secure from all winds and capable of containing 300 sail of shipping. The entrance is exceedingly narrow, and, being covered by very high surrounding lands, the wind always blows either directly in or out. This part is usually called the Narrows, and is well defended by Fort Amherst, mounting 17 guns, and Fort Frederick, mounting 9 guns; there are also two 24-pounders on a platform near the Chain Rock (called Chain Battery) admirably suited for raking an enemy coming in; but this no enemy would be rash enough to attempt, unless they had first secured the new Fort, or Fort Townshend.... This is the residence of the Governor of the island, who is usually a Naval Flag Officer, and who comes out in the spring, and returns before the frost sets in, for England."

The daughter of the chief royal engineer stationed in Newfoundland wrote in her diary in the summer of 1809: "The raging surf of the Atlantic's embrasures of Amherst and Chain Rock batteries, and the line of battleship, as well as the red-sailed fishing skiff come almost within arms reach of the cannon."

Works building was a constant problem for the succession of royal engineers who tried to fortify Signal Hill in the early 19th century. Winter storms undid the previous summer's efforts, England was slow to approve funds, and sometimes it seemed the hill itself rebelled. The hard sandstone resisted scarping, but the hill remained "a naturally strong post," as one engineer reported. "Its rear is secured... by its steepness."

*Plan of the top of
Signal Hill, 1801*

Quecn's Battery, begun in 1796, emerged in the 1830's as the single most important defense work in St. John's. Cannon fire on an approaching ship from this commanding natural shelf would "throw her into confusion and impede her progress at a moment frequently of great interest from the nature of the Entrance."

1810: "...the scarping of the rock on the front or north west side of the hill...has been executing...almost unremittingly during the winter."

1811: "About two hundred Tons of Free Stone of superior dimensions and Quality have been imported from Cape Breton, also about eighty Tons of Stone, from the same Island, procured out of the ruins of Louisbourg fortress."

1811: "The various batteries...are rapidly decaying and whole work becoming more defenceless every year."

1816: "In consequences of the orders received there has been a total suspension of all new works."

1822: "Signal Hill is nearly destitute of defense."

1833: "The Master General and Board have decided, that, everything should be concentrated on Signal Hill; and however unpalatable this decision may be, to the persons whose duty will call them to reside on that spot; yet, except on the score of personal inconvenience, no solid objection can be raised against this decision."

1840: "... in case of an accident occurring during a violent gale or snow storm, the Troops could not venture out of their Barracks for fear of being hurled over the rock."

Recruits, c1800

Signal Hill Tattoo

The defense of St. John's in the late 18th and early 19th centuries relied heavily on volunteer recruits who joined the regular British troops garrisoned at Signal Hill. Attracted by food, clothing, lodging and wages, the fishermen of St. John's willingly joined up for the winter, but desertion was a common problem for the military during the fishing season. Manpower shortages affected both military construction and trade, the lifeblood of the growing town. While the merchants depended on soldiers to protect their ships, they did not hesitate to hire recruits to work the vessels—and then complain about lack of protection. Despite harsh punishment for deserters—including flogging and death— and heavy fines for those who harboured or employed deserters, the problem persisted.

Since England financed the St. John's garrison only reluctantly in some years, it is not surprising that the regiments sent there were not always the best the home country had to offer. In 1776, with the American colonies in revolt, the commander in chief of forces in Newfoundland wrote to complain that the company of the Royal Highland Emigrants recently arrived were in general old, infirm and undisciplined. Other commanders made similar complaints.

When Ireland rose in rebellion against British rule, authorities in Newfoundland worried about the loyalty of the volunteer regiment—and with good reason. Many of the inhabitants were Irish, or of Irish descent, and Roman Catholic. Laws restricting the practice of their religion were relaxed in 1784, but resentment still simmered. The military governor doubted whether the Royal Newfoundland Regiment could be depended on in cases of civil disorder.

On the night of April 24, 1800, a mutiny plot was apprehended. Under the Oath of United Irishmen, some 40 soldiers had agreed to meet at the powder shed near Fort Townshend. Five of those captured were hanged at the powder shed. In 1802 the volunteer regiment was disbanded.

St. John's, 1831, with Queen's Battery in foreground

Shortages of every necessity plagued the soldier's life at St. John's. Hastily built and in short supply, barracks were typically uncomfortable and overcrowded. There never seemed to be enough firewood, coal or candles, eating utensils or bedding. Soldiers often wore their regimental uniform for ordinary work, despite orders, because they had no other clothing. When chronic food shortages got desperate, not only were troops' provisions decreased, but the allowance for wives and children of married soldiers were cut off.

By 1842, Signal Hill was home to about half the entire St. John's garrison. Besides daily exercise and drilling, the soldiers quarried and hauled rock for "the King's works," cut wood for heat and timber, transported provisions, and cleared the parade ground of snow in winter and stones in summer. The soldiers also served St. John's as firemen and as auxiliary civil police (much in demand at election time).

Signal Hill may have been a tolerable home in summer, but even ordinary tasks became fatiguing and sometimes deadly under the weight of winter. Heavy watchcoats and extra fuel were supplied for sentry duty, but "the sentinel was not infrequently found frozen to death," as one commander wrote. "Deep snow and high drifts debarred, during the long winter months ...all field exercise to the troops."

Up to 192 men lived miserably in damp, smoky stone barracks built on the eastern extremity of Signal Hill, its most exposed ridge. On January 10, 1842, "twenty men of that fine Company were reduced to such a state of suffering...owing to the state of their barracks rooms, as to be rendered unfit to duty, 15 of them being sent to Hospital." Officers' barracks on the same ridge remained unoccupied.

Soldiers' belongings

St. John's Harbour, 1842

"We beg leave further to State to Your Royal Highness," residents wrote to Governor Duckworth in 1811, "that the town of St. John's, with the exception of one house, is built of wood; that all our streets are narrow and unlighted; that during three months of the year owing to the severity of the climate, we are shut out from all intercourse with our neighbours. In addition to these circumstances which we are sure will forcibly impress themselves upon the benevolent mind of Your Royal Highness, we have to state that we are without a police, without a public establishment for the education of our youth, without a marketplace, and without any legal provision for the poor."

Irish immigrants, starving at home, were beginning to swell the population. From 3,400 in 1800, it jumped to 10,000 by 1830—but the town still looked like a large fishing village. A visitor around 1840 wrote that fishermen's houses were often "little more than unpainted cottages scattered everywhere."

It wasn't until 1813, two centuries after British planters first began to live in Newfoundland, that residents of St. John's could legally purchase land, build homes or even repair them without first having to secure permission from the governor.

Property grants had been given only to merchants for the fishery, and then only on the waterfront, which meant "no remuneration can be given in lieu of lands taken for public use." Exceptions were made, however, as Joan Vinnicomb found in 1796. Living on what is now Signal Hill Road, she received a grant of land to compensate her when the road from Fort William to Signal Hill went through the property which had been in her family "beyond memory."

With these restrictive laws relaxed, the look of the town changed dramatically. Returning to St. John's after 18 years, Governor Gower was "forcibly struck" to see "that the north side of the harbour is now taken up with Merchants' Stores & Wharfs for the purposes of trade, and the Fishing Stages with many of the Flakes, and other erections for curing fish, removed to make room for them."

St. John's, c1875

With the increase in population and the number of wooden buildings came an increased concern about fire. In 1811, concerned citizens wrote: "Imagination could not portray a more dreadful picture of human misery than would be realized were this town in the depth of winter to become prey to conflagration." Their fears were realized when fire destroyed the town just five years later, and again in 1817 and 1819. Another fire in 1846 levelled 2,000 homes. Fire struck again, most recently, in 1892. This photo shows the aftermath of that vicious blaze which spread from a western section of the city to buildings on Signal Hill.

Sir Thomas Cochrane

Newfoundland got its first civil governor with the appointment of Sir Thomas Cochrane in 1825. Remembered by Historian D.W. Prowse as "the best governor ever sent to Newfoundland," Cochrane initiated a Supreme Court, promoted road-building, education and farming. He recommended the establishment of a university and a municipal council for St. John's.

Cochrane is also remembered for his lavish expenses and sumptuous style of living. He made a pet project of the construction of a massive stone Government House, replacing the old wooden governor's residence. He insisted on extensively altering the plans during construction, until the project consumed all the energies of the Royal Engineer between 1827 and 1831. While plans for the fortification of Signal Hill were frustrated, masons were building Government House of the rough, red sandstone which had been quarried from the slope behind Waldegrave Battery, on Signal Hill.

Except for a flurry of activity during the American Civil War (when it was briefly feared Britain would be drawn into the fighting), the Signal Hill defenses continued to decline. Newfoundland had been granted responsible government in 1855, and England was moving to have all her self-governing colonies look after their own security.

Over vigorous protests from the colonial government, which depended on the garrison for internal order, and from the St. John's merchants who were upset about

View of St. John's Harbour, c1866

losing valuable military contracts, the last of the garrison boarded a troopship bound for Bermuda on November 8, 1870.

As the military presence waned, civilian uses of Signal Hill grew. By the middle of the 19th century, users of the signaling service between the hill and port were exclusively commercial, although the military continued to carry out the service until 1870. Upkeep of the 1815 blockhouse fell to the colony, however, as did the construction of a new signal station, built on the same site in 1859. Flags flying, it appears in the lower left corner of this engraving. Businesses in the expanding mercantile centre of St. John's paid an average of 40 pounds each per year to defray the operating costs.

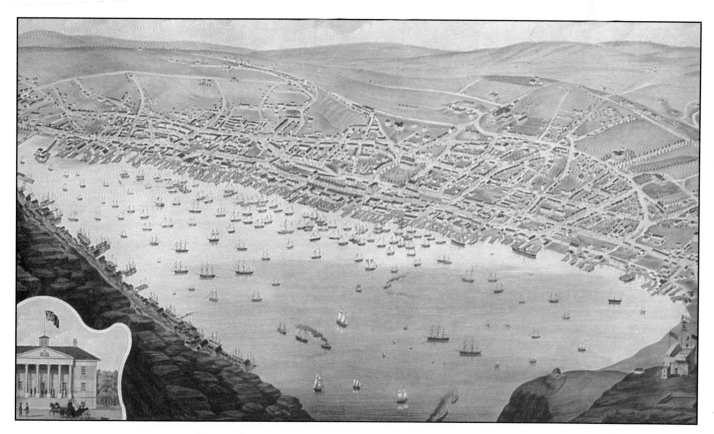

St. John's, 1879

Code of ships' signals, c1800

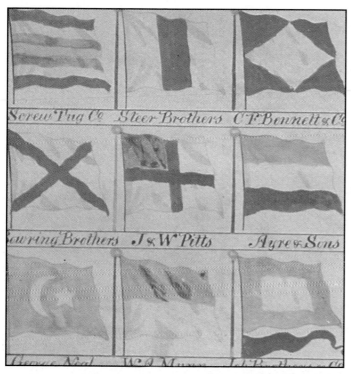

St. John's signal code, 1909

The first building constructed on the summit of Signal Hill, the 1796 blockhouse, was used primarily for signalling the arrival of ships. A century and a half later, when the practice of flying house flags was discontinued, the system had changed little.

A dutyman stationed on the hill kept watch out to sea with a telescope, signalling the approach of a vessel with flags hoisted on a signal mast and yardarm. Each mercantile firm had its own house flag. When spotters in the offices along the waterfront saw their colours raised,

they called for the dock to prepare for the ship's arrival.

A red and white checkerboard meant the vessel belonged to the McBride and Kerr; a blue flag with a white cross said the ship was Duder's; ships owned by W. & G. Rendell flew a red flag with a white dot in the centre. A signal chart from around 1800 shows 39 house flags in all. Other flags warned the firm if the vessel was in distress or if there was illness on board. By the mid-19th century a telegraph station at Cape Spear gave advance notice to the Signal Hill watch that a ship was on its way to St. John's.

As long as the military supplied the service, the signalman followed a code of flags and balls to announce the arrival of foreign vessels as well. By the number of flags and balls and their position on the signal mast and yard arm, the garrison could know if the ship was from Spain, Halifax or New York, if she was a warship or a packet, neutral or enemy.

One of the great public events in St. John's was the sailing of the sealing fleet to the ice each spring. In the middle of the 19th century, when the annual hunt reached its peak, thousands of men from all over the island poured into town in hopes of getting a berth on one of the dozens of ships which crowded the harbour waiting for the signal to sail. However cold that March day, the whole town turned out to send off the fleet. Crowds assembled on Signal Hill to cheer the ships off through the Narrows.

Out on the ice-packed waters of the Labrador Sea and the Gulf of St. Lawrence, the sealers would risk their lives for the $70 to $80 they would earn if their voyage was successful. The huge crowds who gathered again on Signal Hill towards the end of April to welcome the sealers home were not just straining to see which ship would be the first back, but also which ships returned at all. Of the first 50 steamers to go to the hunt between 1863 and 1900, 41 were lost at sea. The number of sailing ships which went down in the ice has never been counted.

The noonday gun atop Signal Hill

"You will be surprised to hear they have no town clock," Sister Magdalene O'Shaughnessy, one of the founding sisters of the Presentation Order in Newfoundland, wrote home to Ireland in 1833; "the reason given is, that it could not be kept regular in consequence of the extreme cold, so that the only way they have of regulating the time is by the discharge of guns which are fired at stated times during the day."

A noon gun has been fired daily from Signal Hill with few interruptions since the early 1800's. It was silenced on Sundays briefly in 1906 when certain clergymen complained that their sermons were disrupted by the rustle of people checking their pocket watches.

The Signal Hill cannon used to be fired to announce that the day's weather was fair enough for the Regatta to take place on Quidi Vidi Lake. It is uncertain when the annual rowing race, which claims to be the oldest continuing sporting event in North America, was first run, but it may have been as early as 1818. Today it is held on the first Wednesday of August, or the first fine day thereafter.

Naturally enough, Signal Hill itself has long been a great playground for St. John's. In winters past, skaters braved the cold to enjoy the view from George's Pond and Deadman's Pond. In summer, the heights were a popular place for Sunday walks, picnics and berry-picking. As far back as 1901 *The Evening Telegram* reported that Signal Hill was one of "the most frequented resorts for the many tourists who visit our city."

When the imperial garrison left St. John's in 1870, the old wooden buildings it left on Signal Hill were "completely in ruins and utterly useless." But the colony made use of two 30-year old masonry barracks on the hill as hospitals.

"Alterations have turned the gloomy barrack rooms into spacious and airy wards," and what began as the military hospital at George's Pond (but was used instead as barracks because smoke tended to back up into the rooms) became St. George's Hospital. Pictured here around the time of the transition from military control, St. George's had 35 beds and served as a fever or quarantine hospital.

Conditions for patients were not much better than they had been for soldiers. The well tended to freeze in winter and dry up in summer. Snow and rain leaked in from the old roof. Raw sewage from the building seeped out of above-ground pipes on its way to a nearby bog, threatening to contaminate sheep and cattle which grazed in the vicinity. The raging fire of July 8, 1892, which consumed two thirds of St. John's, destroyed St. George's.

George's Pond Hospital, c1870

"The hospital is not as sheltered as could be wished," a special public health commission advised in 1910, but "the absence of dust and smoke and the pure air, are no doubt calculated to be of very great benefit to consumptives."

Tuberculosis (responsible for 20 percent of all deaths in Newfoundland in 1909), diphtheria, smallpox and cholera sent many of their victims into quarantine atop Signal Hill between 1870 and 1920. Fresh air and isolation were primary treatment for these highly contagious diseases, and Signal Hill had plenty of both. Of 249 diphtheria cases treated at St. George's Hospital in 1889, 20 died.

Following the loss of St. George's, the focus of health care on Signal Hill shifted to the old stone barracks on the exposed eastern ridge of the summit, the same building which had given the military men who lived in it so much trouble. The Signal Hill Hospital, as it became known, also served primarily as a quarantine facility.

Weather continued to hamper efforts to put the ill-placed barracks to good use. A savage gale in December of 1890, for example, unroofed the hospital and blew down some of its chimneys. In later years the hospital

Signal Hill Hospital, 1901

staff agreed, for safety's sake, that no one would attempt the walk up or down the hill alone. When a defective chimney in the hospital caught fire on a December evening in 1920, the fire department found the road typically impassable, and the building was lost in the spectacular blaze.

The only new hospital built on Signal Hill in this period was constructed in 1892 in response to a cholera scare. The disease was raging in Europe and, with cases being reported on the east coast of the United States. St. John's wanted a quarantine station for any local cases. It was located in Ross's Valley, the seaward barrens below the summit, the idea being that any cholera victim coming into port would disembark at Chain Rock and be transported around the base of Signal Hill to the hospital. The scare never materialized and the building was used only twice, for smallpox. When vandals set fire to it in 1911, the isolated structure burned to the ground.

Cabot Tower, opened on June 20, 1900, was born in a storm of controversy. Conceived as a celebration of the 400th anniversary of Cabot's much-disputed landing at Newfoundland, and of Queen Victoria's Diamond Jubilee, the tower was to serve as a 24-hour signal station and weather observatory. It would stand on the summit of Signal Hill, replacing a temporary blockhouse erected after the 1859 building burned in a gunpowder explosion.

A.A.Parsons, editor of *The Evening Telegram*, liked the idea of "an imposing edifice to greet the first gaze of the mariner; something worthy of an important seaport like St. John's." But correspondent Arthur English likened the grand project to "the placing of a silk hat on the head of a man who had not a decent pair of boots to keep his feet warm." Parsons later changed his mind and suggested that an insurance system for fishermen and their families would be more fitting. Others felt the money, all

The laying of the cornerstone for the Cabot Memorial Tower

from public subscriptions, should go towards a hospital or a public market.

The laying of the cornerstone on June 22, 1897 by Bishop Howley (a leading proponent of the tower project), was part of two days of festivities and a huge display of national pride. "The entire stock of national flags has been bought up," *The Evening Telegram* reported, "bunting is at a premium, and even the millinery stores are getting ransacked for fancy fabrics and feathers suitable for decorative purposes."

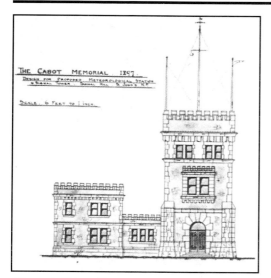

Plan of Cabot Tower

Construction did not begin for another 13 months, and only one of the four turrets in the original design by architect W.H. Greene was ever built. The walls of the gothic revival structure are two feet thick all around and built of Signal Hill's red sandstone, most of which is said to have come from the ruins of st. George's Hospital.

The stonemason at Cabot Tower was Samuel Garrett, who himself lived in a slate house he built on Duckworth Street. While working on the tower, he apparently took advantage of bad weather and leftover stone to build four small attached houses on Temperance Street, near the base of Signal Hill—one for each of his daughters.

Just after the opening of Cabot Tower, Judge D.W. Prowse, one of the chief promoters of the tower, wrote in the *Daily News*, "Let us hope that with the new signalling system in force the lives of our hardy fishermen and sailors will, in the future, be much better protected and cared for than they have been in the past."

Guglielmo Marconi, who received the world's first transatlantic wireless message at Signal Hill in 1901, was born in Bologna, Italy, 27 years previously. James Clerk Maxwell had just developed the theory of electromagnetic waves, and Heinrich Hertz actually generated and detected the waves in 1888, when Marconi was 14 years old. The young boy took great interest in Hertzian waves, joining other scientists who saw they could be used to communicate over distance without wires.

Over the next few years, several inventors made important advances in technology—receivers, tuners and generators—which brought the dream of wireless communication closer to reality. Marconi's goal was to improve the existing technology so that messages could be received at great distances. He did not believe the theorists who said that electromagnetic waves, like light, could not bend around the surface of the earth.

After a successful transmission over 1¾ miles, Marconi moved to England, where there seemed to be more interest in his achievements, and won the world's first patent for wireless telegraphy. In 1897 he founded the Wireless Telegraph and Signal Company Limited and two years later sent a message 32 miles across the English Channel. In another four years he would sit for a photographer in an empty wing of Signal Hill Hospital, waiting to receive a simple signal coming from 1,250 miles away.

The cable ship GREAT EASTERN, at Heart's Content, Newfoundland.

Transatlantic communication had been possible since the 1850's when undersea cable linked England, Newfoundland and mainland North America. Laying thousands of miles of electrical cable was a massive job, and most countries involved had granted monopolies to telegraph companies to protect their investments. The Newfoundland government, for example, had given a 50-year monopoly on cable landings to the Anglo-American Telegraph Company in 1854.

Marconi anticipated that the undersea cable companies would not lightly accept his competition. The first transatlantic cable link had cost $14 million, while he was attempting to make the same connection, without wires, for about $250,000. Telegraph company stocks fell sharply with the news of his success at Signal Hill, and the Anglo-American Telegraph company threatened the young Italian with court action if he received any more telegraph messages from outside Newfoundland.

Marconi did not originally plan to conduct his experiment at Signal Hill. He built two giant stations, each to transmit and to receive, one at Poldhu, Cornwall, and the other at Cape Cod, Massachusetts. Unfortunately, violent storms toppled both stations within weeks of each other, forcing him to change his plans.

To save time and money, Marconi decided to rebuild a simpler one-way transmitter at Poldhu and to send his message to the nearest landfall in North America. St. John's being some thousand miles closer to England than Cape Cod, Marconi sailed for Newfoundland at the end of November with two assistants, P.W. Paget and G.S. Kemp. They checked into the Cochrane Hotel and concealed the real purpose of their arrival, saying they were in St. John's to investigate the possibility of establishing a ship-to-shore wireless station at Newfoundland.

Receiving apparatus

"After taking a look at various sites which might prove suitable, I considered the best one on Signal Hill, a lofty eminence overlooking the port and forming a natural bulwark which protects it from the fury of the Atlantic winds," Marconi wrote. "On top of the hill is a small plateau some two acres in extent which seemed very suitable for the manipulation of the balloons and kites. On a crag of this plateau rose the new Cabot Tower, erected in commemoration of the famous Italian explorer John Cabot and designed as a signal station. Close to it was the old military barracks, then used as a hospital. It was in the forum of this building that we set up the apparatus and made preparations for the great experiment."

Signal Hill was also a good site because there was no iron in the rock to interfere with the electromagnetic current. Marconi had lost the balloon used to hold up the antenna wire to high winds, but managed to fly a kite for the same purpose "in spite of a gusty gale."

"The critical moment had come, for which the way had been prepared by six years of hard and unremitting work, despite the usual criticisms levelled at anything new. I was about to test the truth of my belief.

"Before leaving England I had given detailed instructions for the transmission of a certain signal, the Morse telegraphic "S"—three dots—at a fixed time each day beginning as soon as word was received that everything at St. John's was in readiness. If the invention would receive on the kite-wire in Newfoundland some of the electric waves produced, I knew that the solution of the problem of transoceanic wireless telegraphy was at hand."

On December 12, 1901, Marconi cabled Poldhu to begin transmitting. "Suddenly at about 12:20 p.m. unmistakably three scant little clicks in the telephone receiver sounded several

Marconi's assistants preparing to fly kites

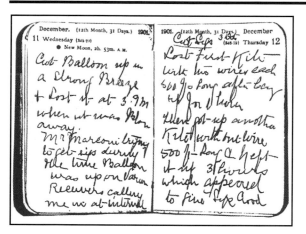

Marconi's diary

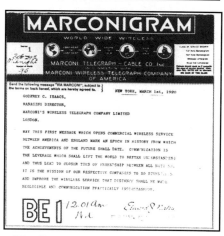

The first commercial wireless message

times in my ears, as I listened intently. But I would not be satisfied without corroboration.

" 'Can you hear anything, Kemp?' I said, handing him the receiver. Kemp heard the same thing that I did, and I knew then that I was absolutely right in my anticipation. Electric waves which had been sent out from Poldhu had traversed the Atlantic, serenely ignoring the curvature of the earth which so many doubters considered would be a fatal obstacle. I knew then that the day on which I should be able to send full messages without wires or cables across the Atlantic was not very far away. Distance had been overcome, and further developments of the sending and receiving apparatus were all that was required."

Strong winds and bad weather defeated Marconi's attempts to strengthen reception of the signal over the next two days. Finally he cabled the news to his London office. *The Evening Telegram* reported, "The old Atlantic cable heard the news, quivered and groaned." With his application to erect a permanent wireless station in Newfoundland blocked by the Anglo-American Telegraph Company, Marconi left for friendlier ground. He had been in St. John's all of 14 days.

Glace Bay, Cape Breton Island, was the site of Marconi's first North American wireless station, established in 1902. Even when the Canadian Marconi company opened its station on the second floor of Cabot Tower in 1933, transatlantic messages were relayed through the Glace Bay station.

The Cabot Tower station served as an important communication link with Labrador summer fishing stations, year-round settlements and communities in northeastern Newfoundland. It also informed ships in the area of local ice conditions, listened to distress signals and helped guide vessels into the harbour in fog. The Marconi station operated alongside the visual flag signalling at Cabot Tower until 1958, and for two years after.

England's declaration of war on Germany on August 4, 1914, caught Newfoundland by surprise, but once again conflict in Europe revived the military role of Signal Hill.

Newfoundland's first response to the war was to recruit support for the Allied troops. Of the 5,482 volunteers who formed the Royal Newfoundland Regiment, 1,300 died and 2,314 were wounded.

The home defense, which the Newfoundland Patriotic Association began organizing in the summer of 1915, has several historic parallels. British naval power was to serve as Newfoundland's first line of defense. Many of the local naval reservists who were to help patrol the long coastline and protect fishing vessels on the Grand Banks were themselves away at the fishery when the call went out. Ice could be counted on to prevent an attack in winter, authorities said, and a local volunteer force would have to be raised after the last of the Regiment went overseas. Watches were stationed on Signal Hill, and in October, 1916, a log boom was erected across the narrows.

The only one of the old harbour works reactivated during the First World War was Waldegrave Battery, just above Chain Rock at the

'F' Company embarking on H.M.T. CALGARIAN, June 1915

base of Signal Hill. A contingent of the Newfoundland Legion of Frontiersmen, a private organization of former military men, seamen and adventurers, repaired the derelict buildings and staffed the battery. Its armament was a single 12-pounder gun and each man carried a .303 rifle.

Advances in the flight range of military aircraft increased Newfoundland's strategic role in the Second World War, both as a supply base for overseas operations and as a vital part of North America's first line of defense. Since 1934, when England had appointed a commission of government to administer the nearly bankrupt dominion, Newfoundland was again a colony run from afar. Great Britain, Canada and the United States agreed that Newfoundland had to be defended and chose St. John's as the centre of operations. The U.S. and Canada split responsibility for the defence of the capital, with the Americans covering Signal Hill in their zone.

Despite great changes in the technology of warfare, the defense of St. John's in the Second World War replayed familiar themes. Gun batteries were remounted in and around the harbour, the largest at Cape Spear, Bell Island (in Conception Bay), and on both sides of the Narrows. Anti-submarine nets, seen in the photo at above right, were strung across the Narrows to protect ships in the harbour from torpedo attack. (A submarine did fire two torpedoes towards the harbour entrance, but neither made a successful

Anti-torpedo baffles at the Narrows, 1944

St. John's Harbour during WWII

hit.) The Canadians built a new fort at Chain Rock, as a further defence against inner harbour attacks, and camouflaged it to look like part of the fishing village known as the Battery.

On the summit of Signal Hill the Americans mounted anti-aircraft artillery, demonstrating in the process that the hill's adaptability was the key to its survival as a strategic site for St. John's over a period spanning three centuries.

Of the early military buildings on Signal Hill, only the imperial powder magazine remains. Built in 1798, the low stone building had been substantially renovated twice this century. The first time was in 1919, following an explosion of powder stored there for the noonday gun. More recently, the operators of the Canadian Marconi Company station at Cabot Tower found it useful for storing heating oil, but the structure fell into disrepair. Since becoming part of Signal Hill National Park in 1958, the magazine has been restored.

The old masonry barrack at the Queen's Battery survived until 1961. The barrack served as a permanent residence for the signalmen on the hill after the military vacated it. From 1939 until the park was established, a government-appointed caretaker lived in the building with his family. By this time the original stone face had been covered in clapboard, but any plans to restore the old barrack were lost with the fire which took the building.

Besides their renewed military use in this century, buildings at Waldegrave Battery have served variously as a dance hall, an explosives storehouse for local importers and, ultimately, a source of stone for other

Queen's Battery barrack, c 1959

buildings in the city. After the war, residents of Signal Hill and the Battery area were permitted to dismantle the World War I fort. The stone turned up in new foundations for their homes and in a wall around the Newfoundland Hotel. The Church of England later received permission to remove the remaining stone for use in repairs to its cathedral in St. John's.

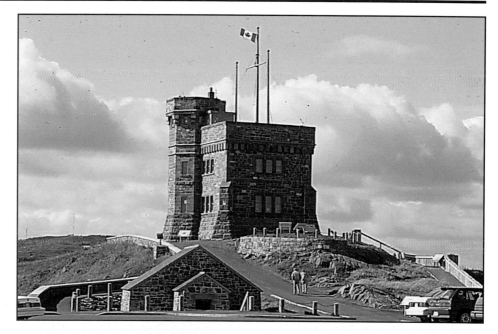

Signal Hill was "One of the first sights to be visited by almost every tourist," reported *The Evening Telegram* in 1930. The newly formed Newfoundland Tourist and Publicity Commission had rounded up six old British cannons and mounted them at the Queen's Battery. This was the first historical restoration effort in Newfoundland.

After Newfoundland joined Canada in 1949, the then-editor of the paper, C.E.A. Jeffrey, successfully pressed the case for Signal Hill to become a National Historic Park. Celebrated as the site of the last battle (in 1762) of the Seven Years' War, Signal Hill was declared a National Historic Park on May 22, 1958. The second largest in Canada, the park covers 642 hectares of dramatic landscape and includes the remains of nearly three centuries of tentative human occupation.

Some of the ruins have been stabilized, and plans call for the restoration of the Queen's Battery. From the summit of Signal Hill, the outlines of fields are still visible in Ross's Valley, where military tradesmen lived with their families and kept animals and garden plots in the 19th century. The foundation of the cholera hospital stands out among the grasses. Along the sides of sea-facing hills are the bits of wall built into the cliffs to reinforce their natural steepness against scaling by an enemy. Everywhere are the marks of people's efforts to alter Signal Hill, but even so, even now, much of the hill is wild again.

Cover
Signal Hill scene
Painting by William Hayward,
c 1904
Mrs. Irene Angel

6 Signal Hill
Photograph; Cam Mustard,
1982

8 **Left**
St. Brendan and his fellow
monks
Illustration; University of
Heidelberg
Right
Early navigation techniques
Woodcut; Zentralbibliothek,
Solothurn, Suisse

9 **Right**
John Cabot
Imaginary portrait by C.B. Pezzi,
1881

10 Albert Cantino's map, 1502
Public Archives of Canada

11 **Left**
Lisbon, c 1500
Engraving; Bibliothèque
Nationale, Paris
Right
Codfish, 1910
Photograph; Public Archives of
Canada

12 **Left**
Dried salt cod
Photograph; Barrett / Photon

Right
Fishing, curling and drying cod,
c 1700
Engraving; Public Archives of
Canada

13 Sir Humphrey Gilbert
Engraving; Metropolitan Toronto
Library

14 Map of Plaisance, c 1660
Public Archives of Canada

15 **Left**
John Guy
Painting; Newfoundland Museum
Right
Capture of St. John's, 1696
Engraving; Bibliothèque
Nationale, Paris

16 **Left**
Batholomew (Black Bart) Roberts,
c 1700
Engraving; National Maritime
Museum, London
Right
Paterero
Photograph; Barrett/Photon
Signal Hill National Historic Park

17 View of Signal Hill and Narrows,
c 1750
Painting; Newfoundland Museum

18 **Left**
Lieutenant-Colonel William
Amherst, c 1760,
Webster, J.C.: The Recapture of
St. John's, 1762

19 Chart of St. John's Harbour, 1798
Public Archives of Canada

20 **Left**
View of the Narrows, 1798
Painting by E.P. Brenton
British Library Board
Right
Amherst's Tower, c 1790
Public Archives of Canada

21 **Left**
Plan of the top of Signal Hill,
1801
Public Archives of Canada
Right
Signal Hill Tattoo
Photograph; Donald Lane
Courtesy McDonald's Restaurants

22 **Left**
Recruits, c 1800
Newfoundland Museum
Right
Signal Hill Tattoo
Photograph; Donald Lane
Courtesy McDonald's Restaurants

23 **Top**
St. John's, 1831, with Queen's
Battery in foreground
William Edgar
Public Archives of Canada
Bottom
Soldier's artifacts
Photograph; Barrett/Photon
Signal Hill National Historic Park

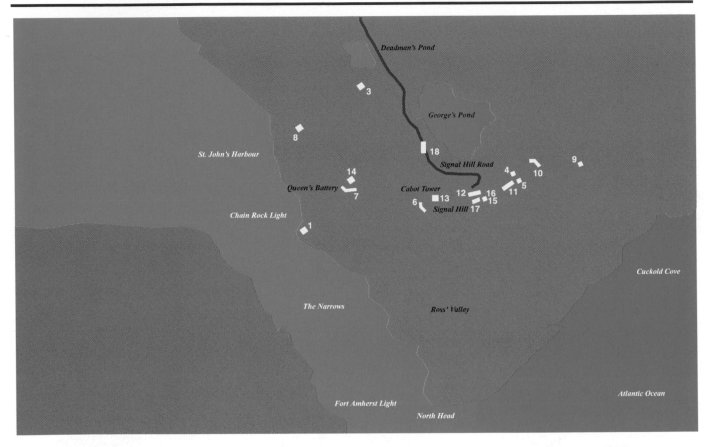

1.)	Chain Rock Battery, 17th century	7.)	Queen's Battery, 1796	13.) Blockhouse, 1815
2.)	Fort Amherst, 1771	8.)	Waldegrave Battery, 1798	14.) Queen's Battery Barracks, 1831
3.)	Wallace's Battery	9.)	North Point Battery	15.) Stable, 1835
4.)	Blockhouse, 1795	10.)	North Battery, 1798	16.) Officers' Barrack, 1836
5.)	Barrack, 1796	11.)	Soldiers' Barrack, 1800	17.) Soldiers' Barrack, 1837
6.)	Duke of York's Battery	12.)	Officers' Barrack, 1804	18.) George's Pond Hospital

Photo courtesy Ben Hansen, 1997